T0333652

Supporting Childhood Obesity in Schools: A Guidebook for *Down Mount Kenya on a Tea Tray*

This guidebook, designed to be used alongside the storybook *Down Mount Kenya on a Tea Tray*, has been created to inform readers about the physical, social and psychological impacts of childhood obesity.

Created for busy parents, teachers and professionals, this book is founded upon recent research and written in an engaging and accessible style. Chapters explain the surprisingly complex causes of childhood obesity and highlight that children often have little control over the factors that may lead them to become obese. The physical and psychological consequences of obesity are explored and strategies suggested, ranging from individual and family support to changes that need to be made at a societal level to tackle this significant public health issue.

Key features include:

- an accessible guide to childhood obesity
- chapter-by-chapter discussion points for use with *Down Mount Kenya on a Tea Tray* to encourage open and honest conversations about childhood obesity and its effects
- strategies to support obese children and their families to sustain positive lifestyle changes.

This is an essential resource for parents, teachers and other professionals looking to understand childhood obesity and support children aged 8–12.

Plum Hutton is a chartered educational psychologist and former learning support teacher. She holds a doctorate in educational psychology. She has more than 15 years of experience working as a local authority educational psychologist and latterly has transferred to independent practice. Through her work she has pursued and delivered training on many areas of professional interest, including supporting children with persistent anxiety, attachment difficulties, literacy difficulties and sensory processing differences.

Plum is a keen storyteller. She has gathered inspiration for her writing from her work, the challenges of parenthood and also through a nomadic existence as an Army wife, which has taken her to many locations across the UK and as far afield as East Africa.

Kate Rennie is a GP, working within the NHS and Army medical services. Prior to studying medicine, she completed a psychology degree and also taught primary school age children. The triad of doctor, psychologist and teacher has given her valuable experience, working with children (and adults) in a variety of situations.

She has moved frequently around the UK with her Army husband, settling for a few years to do her medical training in London and then Edinburgh. She currently lives in London, works in Surrey, but travels frequently to Scotland to spend time in the beautiful Scottish Borders.

Adventures with Diversity

An Adventure with Autism and Social Communication Difficulties:
The Man-Eating Sofa Storybook and Guidebook

The Man-Eating Sofa: An Adventure with Autism and
Social Communication Difficulties

Supporting Autism and Social Communication Difficulties in
Mainstream Schools: A Guidebook for *The Man-Eating Sofa*

An Adventure with Dyslexia and Literacy Difficulties:
A Nasty Dose of the Yawns Storybook and Guidebook

A Nasty Dose of the Yawns: An Adventure with Dyslexia and
Literacy Difficulties

Supporting Dyslexia and Literacy Difficulties in Schools: A Guidebook for
A Nasty Dose of the Yawns

An Adventure with Childhood Obesity:
Down Mount Kenya on a Tea Tray Storybook and Guidebook

Down Mount Kenya on a Tea Tray: An Adventure with Childhood Obesity

Supporting Childhood Obesity in Schools: A Guidebook for
Down Mount Kenya on a Tea Tray

Supporting Childhood Obesity in Schools

A Guidebook for
Down Mount Kenya on a Tea Tray

Plum Hutton and Kate Rennie

Illustrated by Freddie Hodge

Routledge
Taylor & Francis Group

LONDON AND NEW YORK

Cover image: Freddie Hodge

First published 2022
by Routledge
2 Park Square, Milton Park, Abingdon, Oxon OX14 4RN

and by Routledge
605 Third Avenue, New York, NY 10158

Routledge is an imprint of the Taylor & Francis Group, an informa business

© 2022 Plum Hutton and Kate Rennie

British Library Cataloguing-in-Publication Data
A catalogue record for this book is available from the British Library

Library of Congress Cataloging-in-Publication Data
A catalog record has been requested for this book

ISBN: 978-1-032-07616-4 (pbk)
ISBN: 978-1-003-20793-1 (ebk)

DOI: 10.4324/9781003207931

Typeset in Antitled and VAG Rounded
by Deanta Global Publishing Services, Chennai, India

Contents

Acknowledgements

We would like to thank:

- Alex Hutton for his patience, optimism and support during the writing of this book

- Thank you to Alex, Will and James Rennie for their encouragement and support.

1. Introduction

This guide is intended to be used with the storybook **Down Mount Kenya on a Tea Tray**, which is an adventure where the protagonist has difficulties due to being obese. The story is likely to appeal to children approximately 8–12 years old. It explores some of the issues faced by pupils who have difficulties with their weight. This includes finding it hard to join in with the physical activities enjoyed by many of their peers, as well as psychological impacts such as social isolation and low mood. Reasons why a child might become obese are highlighted, as well as the challenges involved in trying to make positive lifestyle changes. This practical information is delivered via a fun and adventurous story set in the beautiful, prickly and, at times, dangerous landscape of East Africa.

A Note on the Language Used in this Guide

Obesity is a sensitive subject because it feels very personal to comment on someone's weight. The storybook includes some frank descriptions of an obese child. The portrayal is not intended to make fun of obese children or to judge them. Instead, the aim is to raise awareness of the scale of the issue and the serious psychological and physical impact that obesity can have on children's lives. Therefore, it is argued that it is important to be able to discuss childhood obesity openly and to provide support for children who would like to make positive changes in their lives.

While efforts have been made to provide accurate information in this guide, it is acknowledged that a wide range of research into childhood obesity is continuing to be conducted. Hence, readers are advised to keep up to date with new findings and recommendations.

DOI: 10.4324/9781003207931-1

Synopsis of *Down Mount Kenya on a Tea Tray*

This synopsis may be helpful for adults using this guide who have not yet had the opportunity to read the storybook.

After the sudden death of his mother, 11-year-old Wesley MacKay flies to Kenya to live with his father, Pete. Wesley has never met his father because his parents separated before he was born. Pete is a sergeant in the British Army and he is currently working in Kenya. For Wesley, it is a tremendous shock to lose his mother, move to East Africa and try to forge a relationship with his father. For Pete, it is a shock to discover that he has a son and that he has to take on the role of father when he has no experience of looking after children. The situation is complicated by the fact that Wesley is clinically obese, which sets him apart from his father and the other children at his new school, who are all physically fit and spend much of their time outdoors.

Wesley meets his new classmates, who include Isla Foster (the daughter of Pete's boss) and a boy called Simon. Isla is kind to him, but Wesley takes an immediate dislike to Simon, who appears to be clever, sporty and popular. Wesley is assessed by an army nurse who explains that he urgently needs to lose weight for the sake of his health. So Pete and Wesley endure a trip to the supermarket where Pete endeavours to buy healthy food and Wesley loses his temper. Luckily, they bump into Anna, Isla's mother, who intervenes and plans to take Wesley on a picnic by a river the following day. Wesley is reluctant to go. He wants to be left alone and is frightened of the river. He is surprised to find that he has a good time and loves seeing the Kenyan wildlife. He opens up to Isla and Anna about his life with his mother. He realises that he would like to be able to join in with activities that he can't do because of his obesity and resolves to try to change his lifestyle.

Anna researches childhood obesity and discovers, that in countries where high-energy food is easily available, the majority of the population is at risk of becoming overweight unless they actively take steps to avoid it. Anna resolves to support Wesley and makes a plan to help him to start taking more exercise and to eat more healthily. She encourages Wesley to walk to school, which initially does not go well. Wesley feels very low; he is homesick, grieving for his mother and struggling to adapt to his new diet.

Wesley's class begin planning their end-of-year trip, and Simon suggests climbing Mount Kenya. This would involve five days of high-altitude walking, and Wesley is currently struggling to walk the short distance to school. Wesley picks an argument with Simon and in a fit of anger tells everyone that he is going to climb Mount Kenya.

Wesley and Pete are supported by the Foster family and Anna makes a 'Mount Kenya Plan' with Wesley. It is really tough at first, but Wesley gradually starts building up his fitness and the other children at the school support him. Anna teaches Wesley how to cook. After several months, Pete, Wesley and the MacKays do a practice walk up a mountain that can be climbed in just one day. Wesley finds the walk tiring but copes quite well. The party are caught in torrential rain on their return home and the track collapses beneath their vehicle, rolling the Land Rover upside down. They escape from the vehicle as it fills with flood water, but Anna is badly shaken up. Wesley is glad to be able to comfort her and is buzzing with his walking achievement and adventures.

The teachers hold a meeting for parents to discuss the details of the Mount Kenya trip. Wesley encounters Mr Morgan, Simon's father, who is rude and implies that Wesley will ruin the trip for everyone. Wesley realises that he has misjudged Simon. His father is a bully and Simon is frightened of him.

The children set off on their trip up Mount Kenya and strengthen their friendships through the shared experience. The days are beautiful and the nights camping on the mountain are bitterly cold. On the last night before they attempt to reach the summit, Simon appears to be befuddled, but the others are so cold and tired that they don't notice. They wake before dawn and begin climbing to the summit in the dark, aiming to reach the top at sunrise. Simon is trudging ahead of Wesley when he becomes confused and takes the wrong path. He has altitude sickness but is determined to continue so that he does not disappoint his father. Wesley follows, trying to stop him, and they both fall off the path down a huge precipice. This is not noticed by the rest of the party until they reach the summit and realise that the two boys are missing.

Wesley comes to in the dark, feeling very bruised and sprawled at the bottom of the scree slope. Simon is lying face down in a small lake. Wesley manages to revive him, but Simon has a head injury, a broken arm, is wet and dangerously cold. Wesley tries to keep Simon warm and alert. Wesley talks about his life with his mother and how she suffered from depression and disappeared one evening. The police found her body in a river. When it gets light, Wesley helps Simon back to their campsite and a helicopter takes both boys to hospital in Nairobi. Simon's father initially blames Wesley for Simon's accident, but later realises that Wesley has actually saved his son's life. Wesley returns to school a hero.

The Main Messages in the Story

- The causes of childhood obesity are surprisingly complex. In many countries, there is now easy availability of high-energy food, which is often high in sugar and refined carbohydrates. This, alongside other factors such as genetic susceptibility, mental health issues and an increasingly sedentary lifestyle, has left many people at risk of obesity, unless they actively take steps to avoid it.

- Children typically become obese because of decisions made by the adults in their lives, which in turn are influenced by the culture of the country.

- The risk of children becoming obese may be exacerbated by issues such as loneliness, bullying, depression, bereavement, illness, injury, poor cooking habits and poverty.

- Children who are obese have a significantly increased risk of ill health and psychological problems.

- Making lifestyle changes such as improved diet and increased levels of exercise can have a big impact on childhood obesity. However, making such changes can be tough, especially at first.

- Family, friends, school staff and the wider community can greatly support a child with obesity. Friendships and taking part in social activities are likely to support the young person's mental health and improve their activity levels.

- Setting realistic goals and being supported to achieve those goals may engender a sense of pride and determination. It is acknowledged, however, that Wesley's decision to climb Mount Kenya was a rashly ambitious goal.

2. Understanding Childhood Obesity

What Is Childhood Obesity?

Obesity in children has become a worldwide concern, with more and more children being classified as obese across many nations. It no longer affects only high-income countries: according to the World Health Organization (WHO, 2021a), in 2019 over 38 million children under the age of five years old were classed as overweight or obese worldwide. Almost half of these children live in Asia. In Africa, there has been a 24% increase in children who are overweight in the last 20 years.

The UK government's *Childhood Obesity: A Plan for Action* (HM Government, 2017) states that an estimated one-third of children aged between two and 15 years of age are overweight or obese. This has significant long-term implications for their personal health, as well as other far-reaching effects. Children are becoming obese at a younger age than before and are remaining obese for longer.

There are many ways of describing the concept of obesity, some much more complex than others. A good, simple definition is given by the Childhood Obesity Foundation (2019), where obesity is defined as 'abnormal or excessive fat accumulation that may impair health'. A measure of obesity that has traditionally been used for adults is Body Mass Index (BMI), which enables a person's height-to-weight ratio to be evaluated. The calculation is weight (in kilograms) divided by height (in metres) squared. The agreed cut-off for being classed as obese is a BMI of 30 or over, with a BMI of 32 or over being categorised as morbidly obese. A high BMI score indicates that the body has stored more fat than expected for a healthy life.

The focus of this guide is on children, rather than the adult population. Although BMI is used for children, it isn't quite as clear-cut as it is for adults, as children are still growing. Therefore, their age needs to be

DOI: 10.4324/9781003207931-2

considered as well as their weight and height. Children's levels of body fat should alter with their growth and development. For example, additional body fat is laid down before puberty in preparation for the associated growth spurt.

It is expected that children will become heavier as they grow taller. If their weight is increasing faster than their height, they are likely to become overweight or obese. Growth charts are used to measure this, and most parents will be familiar with these growth charts as they're used in the child health record books (red books) to record babies' weights in the first few months of their lives. There are charts designed for specific age ranges, for both boys and girls, as their expected increases in weight and height do differ slightly. The charts used in the UK are based on the WHO child growth standards charts (WHO, 2021b). Obesity based on these charts is measured using a cut-off value, although these values vary between countries. For example, in the United States, obesity in children is defined as being more than or equal to the 95th percentile of BMI (the top 5%), whereas in Europe it is more than or equal to the 85th percentile (the top 15%) (Sahoo et al., 2015).

Waist circumference is now frequently being used, in association with BMI, to look at a person's risk of future illness. For instance, the higher the waist circumference (often referred to as central obesity), the greater the risk of developing diabetes type 2 or cardiovascular disease.

Wesley's new school in Kenya.

Why Is Childhood Obesity a Concern?

Obesity in children is now so widespread that it is recognised as a crisis or pandemic. Obesity has the potential to cause many problems for the child, which often persist into adulthood, and effect the wider community as described below.

Health problems associated with obesity in childhood:

- An increased risk of developing chronic diseases at a much earlier age than was previously the case.
- Higher than normal blood pressure and cholesterol levels, increasing the risk for cardiovascular disease.
- The risk of developing diabetes mellitus type 2 (which may damage many organs in the body) is seven times higher compared with children of a typical weight (HM Government, 2017).
- Asthma-like symptoms that begin in childhood tend to persist.
- Musculoskeletal problems are increasingly being seen in children, with joints being put under stress due to increased weight.
- It is also known that children who are obese are more likely to have mental health issues, including depression.

Chronic health problems as an adult:

- Obese children are likely to become obese adults, and this brings with it further problems with their health.
- The increased risk of cardiovascular disease and diabetes type 2, along with all their complications, continues into adulthood.
- Breathing difficulties will progress and this may include sleep apnoea, a condition in which a person has episodes at night where they temporarily stop breathing. This needs to be treated with the use of overnight machines to aid breathing.
- There is a higher chance of developing fatty liver disease, gallstones and gastro-oesophageal reflux disease.
- Obesity is also a risk factor for many different types of cancers. The National Cancer Institute (2017) gives some shocking examples: the risk of developing endometrial cancer in women rises with increasing BMI,

with severely obese women being seven times more likely to develop this type of cancer than women with a normal BMI. Other examples include oesophageal, kidney and liver cancers; obese people are twice as likely to develop these types of cancers than those with a normal BMI.

Early disability due to musculoskeletal problems:

- Joint problems starting in childhood continue into adulthood if there are no reductions in weight levels.
- The chance of being in long-term pain or requiring surgery to mend or replace joints is much higher.

Enduring psychological concerns:

- Many psychological issues are associated with obesity including depression, bullying and poor self-esteem. These in turn can negatively affect academic performance.

Increased mortality and reduced quality of life:

- Poor health and/or poor mobility due to obesity can affect people's ability to work and hence their financial security.
- Poor health, chronic pain, lack of employment, low self-esteem and other psychological issues all reduce quality of life.
- There is a twofold risk of dying prematurely, due to the many medical concerns mentioned above (HM Government, 2020).

Economic costs for society:

- Having more people off work and claiming benefits has economic consequences for society.
- Health services are likely to be further stretched as more people require more appointments, more treatment and more surgery.

Perpetuating cycle within families:

- As described by Sahoo et al. (2015), there is evidence that parents who are obese often have children who are obese.

3. The Causes of Childhood Obesity

The general consensus is that obesity is caused by several different factors, some of which play a bigger part than others. Influences can be categorised into three main groups as shown below. However, it is worth remembering that there may be other influences, that are currently unknown or as yet not mainstream ideas. The understanding of childhood obesity continues to evolve.

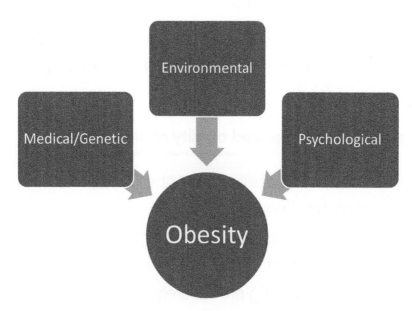

The three main factors that influence childhood obesity.

The factors influencing the development of childhood obesity occur on several levels, ranging from influences on individuals and families to beliefs held by schools, communities and society as a whole. Therefore, a young person will have been affected by everything from their genetic make-up and personality, to values and habits instilled by their family, as well as being influenced by their education and the culture in which they live. Genetic, environmental and psychological influences interact in an individual's life to cause the end result of obesity.

DOI: 10.4324/9781003207931-3

It is important to consider the impact of obesity on the whole population including adults, as there are many similar contributing causes and certainly similar risks and concerns associated with both adult and childhood obesity. However, there is one significant difference. Adults typically are autonomous individuals who make their own choices and their own decisions; usually, they are in control of their lifestyle. Children are moulded and influenced by those around them, particularly their parents or primary caregivers, and the obesity that presents in early childhood is something over which the child has little control.

Childhood obesity is not the child's fault, but the child has to live with the far-reaching consequences of it.

Each of the three main identified areas of influence on childhood obesity will be looked at in more detail below.

Wesley encounters an elephant when on a picnic in the bush.

Medical and Genetic Causes

Research has shown that the majority of people assume that obesity is typically the result of personal choices and free will (Jenkinson, 2020) and therefore many people feel that obesity reflects on the person's character and the decisions they have made. However, it has been shown that genetic predisposition may be a much greater influence on whether a person becomes obese, compared with their choices and the environment in which they live. Studies have investigated identical twins who were separated at birth and matured with the same genes but with different environmental influences. Wardle et al. (2008) demonstrated that identical twins grew up to have remarkably similar BMI and waist circumference measurements even when they were brought up in families with different eating habits, lifestyles and priorities. This strongly suggests that their body shape and weight was significantly affected by their genes. Jenkinson concludes that the risk of children becoming obese is approximately 75% a consequence of their genes – how their bodies are pre-programmed to operate – rather than due to the choices that they make. The home environment is thought to be only about 10% responsible for the development of obesity, with the habits and lifestyle of the culture as a whole having a greater impact. This is daunting when it comes to tackling obesity because there is little that an individual can do to influence the impact of their genes. Throughout history, when food was often scarce, being predisposed to be good at storing surplus energy within the body was likely to be a significant genetic advantage, particularly in times of famine. However, in many countries now, food is consistently plentiful and what used to be a genetic benefit places certain people in the modern world at high risk of developing obesity.

It is often felt that obesity may be a family trait, and it is common for overweight children to also have overweight parents and siblings. There is a genetic component to how the body's hormones and enzymes affect fat regulation and therefore weight gain, although more studies are needed to explore this in greater detail. Even in these cases, genetic factors usually interact with environmental influences as family members are likely to share similar diets and lifestyles. As ever, multi-factorial causation is a significant aspect of childhood obesity.

There are some medical conditions that cause childhood obesity, but it is important to realise that these are very rare. Most of these medical issues have other signs and symptoms, not just weight gain. The majority of them can be excluded through the process of a doctor taking a good clinical history and conducting basic investigations such as blood tests. Only in certain cases would it be necessary to do any more detailed tests to explore a possible medical cause. Some conditions associated with weight gain are not genetically inherited (despite being caused by a person's genes) such as:

- Prader–Willi syndrome
- Turner's syndrome
- Bardet–Biedl syndrome
- abnormalities in specific genes causing problems with hormones or enzymes – for instance, congenital leptin deficiency. Leptin is a satiety hormone, which affects how easily a person feels full after eating (Austin & Marks, 2009).

Thyroid problems can also lead to weight gain and are more common in those who have other family members with similar problems. So they can be said to 'run in the family', but more usually are found in adults: occurring in 1 in 50 adult females compared with 1 in 4,000 babies at birth (Vanderpump, 2011). Thyroid problems often produce a variety of symptoms that manifest themselves earlier than weight gain, so it is less likely to be a cause of childhood obesity than people think. It can be checked on a simple blood test and so is usually excluded by a child's GP.

There are other medical conditions that aren't genetic, such as Cushing's syndrome and polycystic ovarian syndrome (PCOS), which can lead to excess weight gain, but again these are rare in children.

Certain medications can, occasionally, cause weight gain, such as:

- anti-retroviral medication for HIV
- particular anti-depressants
- long-term oral steroid medication
- medication for diabetes, epilepsy or psychosis.

However, they are not typically the cause of obesity in children.

Environmental Causes

Obesity was very rare before and during the Second World War in most parts of the world, although it was noted to be found in the 1930s in many parts of the United States of America. Looking into how environmental influences have changed in recent decades is paramount to find out which of these changes may have contributed to the obesity epidemic. Many studies investigating the increase in rates of obesity have focused on the following two main factors:

- changes in diet
- an increase in sedentary lifestyles.

It is increasingly recognised that changes in countries' culture around food and diet have been instrumental in causing so many people to now weigh more than is healthy for them. Recent evidence suggests that refined carbohydrates, especially sugar, are emerging as the main dietary culprits involved in the rise in levels of obesity in many populations.

Changes in Diet

Until recently, the assumption has been that people were eating more calories than they were using and that the excess calories were stored as fat. The 'Calories-in, Calories-out' message assumes that people were gaining weight largely due to the **quantity** of food that they were eating. Over the last couple of decades, more and more studies have shown that it is not just how much we eat that is causing obesity, but it is **what** is being eaten that is the problem. Changing this belief system is incredibly difficult as the 'Calories-in, Calories-out' message has for a long time been accepted as the reason for people to gain (or lose) weight. However, the situation isn't as simple as that, as is highlighted by the following examples:

- Taubes (2011) describes the Pima tribe from Arizona who are Native Americans. Traditionally, they were labourers, who produced a plentiful supply of their own food. They were physically fit and healthy individuals. From the 1870s, there was widespread famine and the Pima were no longer able to grow enough of their own food. They were given food handouts from the American government. It was noted in the early 19th century that members of this tribe, despite continued high levels of physical work, were overweight. They had gone from eating large quantities of their own-grown food to eating small amounts of predominantly rationed food and yet their weight had increased. The critical factor that had changed in their lives was **what** they were eating. White flour and sugar were large components of the government rations and appear to have been responsible for their weight gain.

- Fung (2016) has explored weight gain in China where traditionally the population was petite, with very few cases of obesity. The introduction of refined sugar in the last couple of decades has led to a significant increase in the number of people who are overweight and obese. Their core diet may not have changed, but a significant change has been the additional intake of sugar.

Refined Carbohydrates and Sugar

Current evidence suggests that it is primarily **what** is being eaten that is driving the obesity crisis, rather than how much we are consuming. Sugar was one of the food groups that was rationed during the Second World War, and children in the 1940s generally ate few sugary products. Over the last few decades, children's exposure to sugar has increased dramatically, with access to sweet food and drinks becoming a regular occurrence. In addition to sugar in its obvious form, highly refined carbohydrates, such as white flour, are swiftly converted into higher levels of sugar within the body than are unrefined sources. Many processed foods consist primarily of refined carbohydrates, and with these being easily available, inexpensive, convenient and tasty, the increase in these foods has led to a rise in sugar consumption in many people's diets.

Many parents may be unaware that the refined carbohydrates in many breakfast cereals and savoury foods such as pizzas, bread and pasta are rapidly converted into sugar by the body. This means that it is possible to consume a high level of sugar without having eaten anything that is obviously sweet. These foods have become staples of many children's diets, and when combined with sugary drinks, snacks, biscuits, sweets, chocolate, etc., children may be exposed to very high levels of sugar on a daily basis. Therefore, there is a correlation between the increase in obesity and the change in diet since the 1940s, from mainly unrefined, homecooked food to highly processed products, made of easily digestible refined carbohydrates. This shift in our society's eating habits is likely to be a significant cause of increased levels of childhood obesity and will particularly impact individuals who are genetically susceptible to weight gain.

This pattern of change is no longer confined to the high-income countries of the Western world. Low- and middle-income countries are unfortunately following the same path.

Insulin Resistance

There are lots of different hormones and enzymes in the human body that are involved in fat regulation. They control how much dietary sugar (from carbohydrates) is used for energy and how much is stored as fat. If that fat-regulation process is not working as well as it should, more of the sugars will be used for storage than for energy, and so a person's weight will increase. One of the hormones responsible for sugar being stored as fat or being used as energy is insulin. Insulin deficiency is the cause of diabetes mellitus type 1 – the problem that is caused by the body not producing any insulin itself, so synthetic insulin is required to be injected to replace it.

It is now known that even in those people who do not have diabetes, one's insulin can cause problems for fat regulation. Too much sugar in the diet produces a rise in the amount of insulin produced by the body, with the result being that the body becomes resistant to the hormone's actions over time, causing more sugar to be used for storage than for energy. This results in weight gain and may lead to type 2 diabetes.

Although there is considerable evidence that a diet high in refined carbohydrates is a leading cause of obesity, the 'Calories-in, Calories-out' argument is still widely believed, as it has been the dominant message to most of the world for many years. New messages, based on recent research, are filtering through to the general public. However, there is still a long way to go before people fully understand that obesity is not simply about eating too much and moving too little, but is the result of a complex process involving many factors including what you eat and when you eat.

Changes in Exercise Patterns

There has been a trend in recent decades of children taking less exercise and living more sedentary lives. Children no longer spend most of their free time playing outside and are less frequently required to do physically demanding chores. Gone are the days when they went off with their friends, only returning home for their dinner. The awareness of stranger danger and increased traffic levels has meant that their freedom to roam has been curtailed. Instead, there has been an increase in structured childcare and after-school activities, with many children being driven around rather than walking or cycling.

There are now lots of opportunities for more formal exercise, with plenty of clubs and activities from which to choose. Unfortunately, these are more easily available for those families who can afford them. The cost of kit and club membership fees, as well as transport costs or giving up parental time, can be prohibitive for many families. The school day can provide opportunities for exercise, either informally at breaktimes or as part of the curriculum, although the time given to the latter has been reduced over recent years. As a response to the reduced levels of exercise, alternative activities have emerged. These tend to be sedentary, especially the use of computer/console games and social media.

Lots of research has been done into how exercise contributes to a person's weight, with more and more evidence emerging that increasing exercise does not necessarily lead to weight loss. The body may adjust its metabolism to cope with the increased energy demands. Fung (2016) gives many examples of how it can be shown that increasing exercise does not equal weight loss. However, exercise is an important part of everyone's lifestyle, particularly if a person is overweight or obese. It definitely needs to be encouraged, but as a contribution to overall health and wellbeing, rather than purely as a weight-loss goal.

Other Environmental Factors

Diet and exercise are always perceived as the major contributory environmental factors for childhood obesity, but others should be considered.

Family modelling is an important determinant of how children eat and what food choices they make. Essentially, children shape their behaviour on what they see their close role models doing. Usually, this would be parents, older siblings and other family members who are involved in the daily life of the child. If these role models frequently graze on sugary snacks, then children are likely to do the same. Their habits typically persist beyond infancy and so the behaviour of family members plays a critical role in determining a child's eating habits.

Socioeconomic status comes with a certain amount of controversy surrounding its contribution to the obesity crisis. It is often thought that more affluent people are more likely to be obese as they can afford to buy more food. As previously discussed, though, it isn't just the amount of food that people eat but also what they eat that causes them to become overweight and then obese. It is now becoming increasingly evident that poorer people are more likely to become obese, certainly in the developed world. In the UK, five-year-olds from low-income families are twice as likely to be obese as those from high-income families, and 11-year-olds are three times as likely to be obese (HM Government, 2017).

A major issue is affordability and availability of the wrong types of food. Filling up children on a tight budget means that refined carbohydrates are likely to make up a large proportion of their diet, with fresh, expensive ingredients being eaten less often. In addition, opportunities for physical activity may be more limited for those in lower-income brackets, due to the prohibitive cost of leisure centre memberships and out-of-school sports activities.

The media influences people in many different ways. Children see television characters as role models and often will copy the behaviour of those they observe on television or social media. Characters making poor food choices are common on television, although the majority of people on television are portrayed as being lean, not fat, which must cause confusion. Adverts aimed at children have focused on highly refined, sugary products – probably encouraging inappropriate food choices – and the labelling of products is confusing. Products may often be identified as being 'healthy', 'low in fat' or 'high in fibre', although a closer look at the ingredients of many of these products will show that sugar is one of the main ingredients, added to make the product more palatable. So, when buying processed food, it can be hard to know whether the product is a healthy choice or not. Although currently problematic, there are significant opportunities for positive change in relation to food advertising and labelling.

There has been a huge increase over the last few years in television programmes about obesity, both reality TV shows and documentaries. A wide range of views have been aired, particularly about the best 'diet' to follow to lose weight, so that the conflicting information has caused confusion. Unfortunately, there has been no consistent message as to what is causing obesity and what can be done about it.

Simon arriving at school by helicopter.

Psychological Causes

While in most cases it is unlikely that obesity is purely caused by a psychological problem, there is a strong association between childhood obesity and mental health issues. Children respond to stress in a variety of ways and may resort to comfort eating when they are upset or sad; they may even control their food intake as a way of managing the lack of control in other areas of their lives. Such behaviours can lead to obesity or the development of eating disorders. In addition, if children see family members eating as a means to relieve stress or depression, then they may do the same.

Although psychological issues such as depression and low self-esteem are closely associated with childhood obesity, it is difficult to establish whether psychological issues **cause** obesity or are a **consequence** of it (Russell-Mayhew et al., 2012). The psychological impact of childhood obesity will be discussed in the following section.

Much more research is needed to explore the causes of childhood obesity, to see if any specific triggers could be influenced to try to prevent obesity from developing in certain children. A longitudinal study currently underway is looking at numerous factors relating to 400 pairs of twins (Momin et al., 2020), which may contribute to our understanding of obesity risks.

4. The Interaction between Psychological Issues and Childhood Obesity

Research exploring the psychological consequences of obesity in children has shown a variety of results, most likely because childhood obesity is such a complex condition that is affected by a range of factors. Rankin et al. (2016) conducted a systematic review of the available studies (between 2006 and 2016), looking into the psychological impacts of childhood obesity. The review concluded that there are definitely several mental health concerns for children who are obese. However, researchers have struggled to differentiate between what is a consequence of being obese and what psychological problems contribute to children becoming obese. The relationship between obesity and psychological problems appears to be bidirectional. Regardless of how the issues develop, it is important to acknowledge that a child who is obese is very likely to have one or more psychological challenges.

It has also been found that adverse childhood experiences may contribute to the risk of children developing obesity throughout their lives (Danese & Tan, 2021). It is thought that this is because the emotional turmoil that they have experienced causes problematic coping responses, stress and disturbances in the body's metabolic processes (Hemmingsson et al., 2014). Therefore, supporting emotionally vulnerable children may be an important component of preventing future obesity.

Some psychological factors associated with obesity are discussed below.

DOI: 10.4324/9781003207931-4

Anxiety, Depression and Self-Esteem

Obese adolescents have been found to have an increased prevalence of anxiety and depression compared with the general population (Roberts, 2021). Many studies demonstrate a link between obesity and depression, and there is evidence that there are increasing levels of psychological distress with higher body weights. The association between anxiety and obesity is less clear, although it has been found that obese girls experience higher rates of social anxiety compared with obese boys (Rankin et al., 2016). There is evidence that older obese children (12–14 years old) have a greater likelihood of developing depression and other emotional issues, such as anxiety and paranoia, indicating that the emotional impact of obesity may become more pronounced through the teenage years (Rankin et al., 2016). In addition, obese adolescents are more likely to be diagnosed with a mood disorder than their typical-weight peers when they reach adulthood.

A review of the literature indicates that childhood obesity has a clear impact on young people's self-esteem, leading to lower perceptions of self-worth and self-competence than children of typical weight. Problems with low self-esteem seem to increase as obese children mature through adolescence (Rankin et al., 2016).

It is clear that obesity, depression and low self-esteem are connected, but the causes of the issues are complex and many factors may be involved. In some cases, childhood obesity is a contributing factor to depression, whereas, in other cases, persistent low mood may cause significant weight gain. Hence, interventions that support mental health are likely to be an important strategy for preventing childhood obesity.

Emotional Regulation and Conduct Issues

Several studies have indicated that infants who have poor emotional regulation and who seek immediate gratification are at higher risk of obesity in later life (Graziano et al., 2013; Smith et al., 2020). For example, Anderson et al. (2017), found that emotional regulation at the age of three was a predictor of obesity at 11 years old. It was found that providing structure, such as regular bedtimes and mealtimes, as well as limits on screen time, led to better emotional control and lower rates of obesity. Similarly, Aparicio et al. (2016) found that stress and poor emotional regulation in childhood were associated with reduced physical activity, comfort eating, disrupted sleep patterns and obesity. It has also been found that pre-school children who prefer instant gratification (rather than being able to wait for a treat) had significantly higher body mass 30 years later (Schlam et al., 2013). Hence, acknowledging that children who are impulsive are at increased risk of obesity could help parents and professionals to work preventatively with this cohort.

Given the links between obesity and impulsivity, researchers have explored whether there is an association between obesity and children with a diagnosis of attention deficit hyperactivity disorder (ADHD). However, the studies report a variety of results, with some showing a link between obesity and ADHD and others reporting no association (Rankin et al., 2016).

Obese adolescents have been found to have a higher prevalence of anger and disruptive behaviour than peers of lower weight (Roberts, 2021). It has been suggested that parents may rely on food as a way to soothe troublesome infants, which, when combined with other factors (such as the child's genetic susceptibility, temperament and levels of impulsivity), may lead to an increased risk of obesity in later life (Smith et al., 2020).

Parental Mental Health and Parenting Style

There is some evidence that there is a link between parental stress and greater weight, as well as unhealthy behaviours in adolescents. There may be an impact even before birth, as maternal distress during pregnancy was later found to lead to higher rates of obesity when the children were ten years old (Smith et al., 2020). Foetuses whose mothers showed raised cortisol levels (an indicator of stress) were found to have higher body mass in the first two years of life (Stout et al., 2015). The links between parental stress and childhood obesity continue after the child is born, as high stress levels in mothers in the first year of the baby's life are associated with higher BMI at five years old (Leppert et al., 2018). Also, maternal stress in mothers of five-year-olds has been found to be a predictor of obesity at 11 years old (Hope et al., 2019).

There is a clear link between maternal depression and childhood obesity (Smith et al., 2020). Parenting is demanding at the best of times. Parents who are struggling with poor mental health may rely more on highly processed fast food/ready meals, rather than cooking fresh ingredients. They may also not have the time and energy to engage in physical activity with their children and to enforce routines and boundaries. It has been shown above that good emotional regulation in children is associated with lower body weight, and caregivers are instrumental in helping children to learn to regulate their emotions. When parents are under stress, it is more difficult for them to support their children with emotional regulation.

Parenting style is also relevant. Authoritative parents, who are supportive and responsive but set their children firm limits, are reported to promote healthier eating habits, higher levels of physical activity and lower BMIs in their children compared with other parenting styles (Sleddens et al., 2011). Parents play a vital role in promoting physical activity, healthy eating and structure within the home (Smith et al., 2017). Supporting parental mental health is therefore likely to be an essential factor in preventing childhood obesity.

Stigmatisation and Bullying

Disapproval of overweight and obese children is common and can increase the child's feelings of body dissatisfaction (Smith et al., 2020). Negative views of childhood obesity are often tolerated within society, due to the misguided belief that shaming overweight children will motivate them to change. Many people assume that the child is responsible for being obese and that their weight is a consequence of poor self-discipline (Browne et al., 2021). However, the reality is that a wide range of factors contribute towards children becoming obese, and many of those factors are not within the child's control.

The stigmatisation experienced by obese young people has been found to contribute to their social isolation, reduced physical activity, unhealthy eating habits (such as binge eating) and higher levels of weight gain (Pont et al., 2017). The views of others actually contribute to the problem. Evidence suggests that overweight children are ridiculed not only by their peers but also by parents, healthcare professionals and school staff (Smith et al., 2020).

These children are often victims of bullying. A study by the World Health Organization (2017) found that obese children experienced a 63% increased chance of being bullied compared with their lower-weight peers. Other studies have shown that children who are overweight or obese are 4–8 times more likely to be bullied than their normal-weight peers (Rankin et al., 2016). Bullying can have significant consequences such as depression, difficulties making friends, conduct problems, poorer school performance and reducing the motivation to change, which may result in more weight gain (Smith et al., 2020).

Young people who are overweight or obese are at high risk of being a victim of bullying, and those most distressed by the bullying show lower self-esteem and a greater incidence of depression. Interestingly, obese children are also thought to be at increased risk of engaging in bullying and victimising others (Rupp & McCoy, 2019). Bullying is a significant factor in the incidence of eating disorders and unhealthy weight-management behaviours as children (particularly girls) mature through adolescence (Rankin et al., 2020). The emergence of cyberbullying has made it especially challenging for adults to prevent the harassment of others, as children can easily contact each other anonymously or indirectly through personal devices (Browne et al., 2021).

The serious impact of stigmatisation of obese children highlights the importance of educating society as a whole about the complex challenges that children with obesity face and the close links that the condition has with mental health issues. Fashion and beauty trends that seem to value exceptionally slim physiques should also be examined to ascertain the impact they have on young people's feelings about their bodies, as overweight and obese children are more likely to show higher levels of body dissatisfaction.

Peers, parents, school staff and healthcare workers should be aware that mocking obese children may not only have a significant negative impact on the child's psychological wellbeing, throughout adolescence and beyond, but may also increase the likelihood of further weight gain. All members of society have a role to play in helping to solve the current obesity epidemic.

The river where Wesley and the Fosters go swimming.

Covid and the Psychological Impact on Obesity

Concerns have been raised about the detrimental impact that the Covid-19 pandemic may have had on young people at risk of obesity. First, it has been found that obesity is a risk factor for serious illness among people who contract Covid-19 (Browne et al., 2021). Therefore, Covid has presented an elevated threat to the physical health of obese people. Second, Covid has led to lockdowns and social restrictions, which have left susceptible children at a heightened risk of developing obesity and mental health issues. Children experienced isolation at home while they were unable to attend school, as well as reductions in social interaction, supervised physical activity and familiar routines (Browne et al., 2021), all of which are protective factors against mental health issues such as depression. Feeling isolated, bored, low and anxious may lead to comfort eating, which may have a negative impact on children's weight. Some children lost the provision of a nutritious meal provided each day at school and had less access to fresh food, as families stocked up on processed foods with long shelf lives.

Storz (2020) suggested that the Covid pandemic created an environment for many children that was unparalleled in leaving them prone to developing behaviours associated with obesity, such as increased sedentary behaviour and screen time, unhealthy food intake and erratic sleep patterns. There is increasing evidence of an association between poor quality of sleep and the development of obesity (Roberts, 2021). This relationship seems to be bidirectional and to be especially prominent in vulnerable adolescents. This is concerning given that a substantial number of adolescents report not having enough sleep to function effectively (Scott, Biello & Woods, 2019).

Rates of domestic violence and child abuse rose during lockdowns (Browne et al., 2021) as families were living at close quarters and under increased levels of stress. For many, it was harder to seek support from health and social care professionals due to the need for social distancing or problems with staff illness. As mentioned above, adverse childhood experiences are known to be associated with an increased risk of obesity in later life.

The Covid-19 pandemic triggered sudden changes in behaviour. It remains to be seen whether new habits caused by temporary lockdowns will become entrenched and lead to a long-term increase in behaviours associated with poor mental health and higher body mass.

Conclusions about the Psychological Impacts of Obesity

When considering childhood obesity, it is often the consequences for physical health that are most apparent. However, there is a very strong association between obesity in childhood and poor mental health. The links between obesity and psychological issues are complex, and it is often hard to determine if obesity causes mental health issues or vice versa. What is clear is that the combined cost of supporting young people with obesity and associated psychological problems is high. The more we, as a society, can do to prevent this situation from occurring, the better. In the meantime, children who are already significantly overweight need to have their psychological concerns acknowledged, taken seriously and addressed appropriately. This may require input from a multi-disciplinary team including medical doctors and dieticians, but also, importantly, psychologists. Support from friends, family, schools and the local community may also be invaluable.

5. Using *Down Mount Kenya on a Tea Tray* to Promote Discussion

Woven into the **Down Mount Kenya on a Tea Tray** story is information about childhood obesity, so children who are struggling with their weight may relate to events in the story. In addition, the story is a useful resource to promote understanding and discussion among children and adults who may not have considered the impacts for children living with obesity.

In this section, questions are posed that could be used to generate discussion about **Down Mount Kenya on a Tea Tray**. This will aid adults to facilitate debate with children, even if the adult has not had the opportunity to read the whole storybook.

Prologue

Wesley flies to Kenya to live with his father, Pete, after the loss of his mother. Pete waits anxiously to meet his son at the airport.

Why do you think social services might have arranged for Wesley to move to live with his father?

- Wesley's mother is no longer able to look after him. We find out later in the story that she has died. Wesley has no other close relatives in the UK who could care for him.

Imagine your feelings if you were told you were moving to East Africa to live with someone you had not met before?

- It would be a very confusing and frightening time. Wesley is grieving for his mother and the loss of everything that is familiar to him – his home, school and country. He has to adjust to living in East Africa and

DOI: 10.4324/9781003207931-5

try to form a relationship with his father who has no experience of being a parent.

Chapter One

Wesley starts attending his new school. Pete explains why Wesley has moved to Kenya to his boss, Major Foster.

Can you remember your feelings when you started something new?

- It is normal to be nervous about not knowing the other children, the school rules and routines, etc. On top of this, Wesley is feeling emotionally very low and is overwhelmed by moving to Kenya.

What are the pros and cons of being different from the other children at school?

- It can be nice to stand out if you are different in a way that is valued, such as being a fantastic gymnast, good at art or tall for your age. However, children often want to fit in with their peers, so being visibly different can make them feel self-conscious and isolated, particularly if their appearance is their defining feature.

How did Isla manage to deal tactfully with the problem that Wesley was too large for the class chairs?

- She saw a solution to the problem and tactfully suggested that the chairs were too small, rather than saying that he was too large.

What do you think Wesley might mean when he thinks that 'his mother hadn't wanted to be his mother'?

- He feels abandoned by his mother and so assumes that he is unlovable and that his mother did not want him. In fact, his mother loved him very much but was struggling with mental health issues.

What are the challenges facing Pete when he agrees to look after Wesley?

- He has no experience of parenting and his parents had not been good role models for him. He has not run his own home before, as he has lived in Army accommodation where all his meals were provided for him. He does not know how to cook. He has to forge a relationship with a grieving, angry boy. He needs to help Wesley to overcome his obesity, and Pete has always led a very active life and has no experience of obesity.

Chapter Two

The Army nurse tells Wesley that he has to go on a strict diet, and he is angry and upset about this. Wesley and Pete argue in the supermarket. Isla's mother, Anna, plans to take Wesley on a picnic.

Simon arrived at school by helicopter. Does that mean his family are very rich?

- Compared with many Kenyan families, Simon's family is very wealthy. However, parts of Kenya are remote and difficult to reach by road, so it is not uncommon for landowners to train as pilots. Simon lives too far away to travel to school by car, particularly in the rainy season when the roads are impassable.

Should the nurse have told Wesley all the health risks of obesity?

- Mary should not have related the health risks associated with obesity so bluntly. She was exhausted and frustrated by Wesley's sullen attitude. She knows he is not directly responsible for his weight. However, her rant does bring home to Wesley that his weight may seriously affect his physical and mental health.

What is a boda boda?

- It is a Kenyan nickname for a motorbike. Another name for a motorbike is a picky picky.

Why do you think UK brands of food are so expensive in the supermarket?

- Because they are usually imported from the UK, which is much more expensive than buying local produce. UK brands are popular with British Army families who like to be reminded of home.

Why do you think Wesley is craving sweet food so much?

- He is used to eating lots of sugary food, so that is what his body is physically wanting. He also craves it psychologically, because he is seeking some familiarity in his life and comfort eating has been his main strategy to help him to feel better when he is low.

Wesley says, 'I don't want to lose weight! I'm just fine the way I am.' Do you agree with him?

- No. His obesity is negatively impacting his life and seriously limiting his ability to engage in activities enjoyed by his peers. It is also a risk factor for long-term psychological and physical problems. However, he is feeling overwhelmed, and staying as he is feels like an easier option compared with losing weight.

Is he likely to be able to change his habits if he doesn't want to change?

- It is hard for someone to sustain long-term change unless they are motivated to do so. It will be really important for Wesley to decide that he wants his life to be different, rather than the adults in his life just telling him to change.

Why do you think that a river would be the last place that Wesley would like to visit?

- The reader is not yet aware that Wesley's mother drowned in a river. He also feels very self-conscious about wearing swimming trunks in front of the Foster family.

Chapter Three

Wesley goes on the picnic with the Fosters and meets some giraffes, zebras and an elephant. He swims in the river and tells Isla and Anna what happened to his mum. He resolves that he wants to lose weight so that he can join in with more activities.

How do you think Wesley felt when he saw the giraffe?

- He was totally awed. He had never left the UK before and had never experienced exciting wildlife, except on television.

The first giraffes that Wesley encounters.

What did Freddie mean when he said, 'Not another zebra crossing!'

- It was a joke because there were no traffic lights, roundabouts or zebra crossings in Nanyuki. However, real zebras did often cross the tracks when the family was driving out in the bush.

Why did Wesley see 'fear and panic' swirling along the riverbed?

- He was imagining what had happened when his mother drowned. Her death has made him scared of fast-flowing rivers, particularly as he is aware that he is not a strong swimmer.

Why could Wesley not remember his mother playing with him?

- His mother struggled with depression and often did not have the energy to engage with him. When she did engage, they tended to eat and watch television together, rather than play.

What do you think might have happened to Wesley's mum?

- So far, it has only been explained that Wesley felt horror and despair and that bringing him swimming had not been a great idea. So any number of disasters may have befallen his mother. Some readers may correctly guess that she drowned.

What made Wesley realise that he wanted to lose weight?

- The children at his school in Kenya tended to have active, outdoor lifestyles with lots of sport. Wesley realised that his obesity meant that he could not join in with many of the activities that his peers enjoyed. He was keen to have friends, and a good way to make friends is by doing activities together.

Henry Foster says that solving obesity is simple: 'eat less and exercise more'. Is he right?

- No, it is more complicated than that. It is important to look at the factors that may have caused the person to become obese in the first place, including the culture of the country, availability of food, the type of food that is eaten, sedentary lifestyles and then individual family differences such as genetic predisposition, mental health issues, bereavement, eating habits, etc.

What lifestyle changes have happened in high-income countries in recent years that have left populations more prone to obesity?

- High-energy food is readily available, particularly very processed products that are high in sugar and refined carbohydrates.
- Daily life is more sedentary, with many tasks being undertaken by machines (e.g. washing machines, vacuum cleaners).
- Many more families own a car, rather than walking or cycling.
- Pastimes have become dominated by electronics, such as computer games and television.

Do you think that people make judgements about others based on the way that they look? Are those first impressions accurate?

- We often make assumptions based on people's physical attributes, clothes, hairstyle, race, gender, etc. Humans tend to mentally assign people to categories based on our experience of the world. However, first impressions may be completely wrong and may tell us little about a person's qualities and values.

Does it feel uncomfortable talking about how people look and about being overweight? Should we discuss obesity or not?

- In the UK, many people feel it is fashionable to be slim. It is also considered rude to comment on a person's weight or body shape.

It feels uncomfortable to discuss childhood obesity, especially because it may be assumed that the problem is the child's fault. However, childhood obesity presents a significant health risk and is in most cases preventable. Therefore, it is important that children and families are educated about the causes and solutions.

Chapter Four

Wesley starts trying to take more exercise and to eat more healthily, but the first few weeks are challenging, and he feels low. Simon suggests that the class could climb Mount Kenya as their end-of-year trip. Wesley argues with Simon and rashly tells everyone that he is going to climb the mountain.

Why do you think Wesley wanted to go to sleep after walking to school?

- His body is unaccustomed to taking exercise before school. Walking to school has no effect on Isla, but for Wesley it is very physically demanding and leaves his body feeling tired and sleepy afterwards.

Do you think Simon was intending to be unkind when he suggested that the class climbed Mount Kenya?

- No, he hadn't intended to exclude Wesley from the school trip. He had just forgotten that Wesley wasn't able to do the same activities as the rest of the class.

Is Wesley being reasonable when he argues with Simon? Why do you think he is so angry with Simon?

- No, he is not being reasonable. He interprets Simon's actions as being more negative than they are. Wesley is unhappy, suffering from low mood, anger and grief. He blames Simon for his troubles.

Isla explains that climbing Mount Kenya is a five-day walk. Do you think Wesley is being realistic in saying he will climb the mountain?

- Wesley didn't realise that climbing Mount Kenya was such a big physical challenge. He assumed it was like climbing Mount Snowdon where it is possible to take a train almost to the top. Given his very poor levels of fitness and lack of stamina, it seems very unlikely that he will achieve his goal.

What does Isla mean when she tells Wesley to be nice to Simon and that Wesley is not the only one with problems?

- Isla knows that Simon has difficulties at home that are not apparent at school. Wesley assumed that Simon's life was perfect and that his own life was rubbish by comparison. Very few people have perfect lives. There is usually some good and bad in all lives.

Chapter Five

Anna teaches Wesley to cook some meals, and he perseveres with walking to school. It is a difficult few weeks, but he starts to lose weight.

Do you think Wesley will be able to make the changes needed to be able to climb Mount Kenya?

- It will be a huge challenge, which will involve a public loss of face if he does not achieve it. It is also difficult for the teachers, as they know that Wesley is unlikely to be able to complete the trip. He will need considerable support to achieve this goal.

How is learning to cook helpful?

- It helps Wesley to feel in control over what he eats and to engage positively with food.
- It allows him to eat a range of nutritious ingredients, rather than highly processed food.

- It teaches Wesley a skill so that he can begin to be 'the expert' in cooking certain meals, rather than Pete always having to take charge and not doing a very good job. This improves his relationship with Pete as cooking starts to be an activity that they do together.

Why were mealtimes a battleground in the first few weeks that Wesley lived with Pete?

- Wesley was resisting eating more healthy food, and Pete felt completely out of his depth in trying to properly cook for the first time in his life. Wesley was unhappy and angry, and they were struggling to form a relationship with almost no common interests or shared experiences. Therefore, mealtimes typically led to arguments.

Chapter Six

Wesley develops his fitness by running daily at school. He apologises to Simon. Wesley, Pete and the Fosters plan a hike up the Aberdare Mountains.

What do you think helped Wesley to keep doing a daily run at breaktimes?

- The support of Mr Mwangi and the other children was a great help so that he was not running alone. Also, everyone knew about the goal he had set himself. This added an element of peer pressure to his training and loss of face if he gave up.

What do you think might be the problem with Simon?

- Simon never talks about home and is very relieved to leave his father when he is dropped off at school. He also becomes anxious about class tests and performances. It has not been explained to the reader yet, but Simon is under huge pressure at home.

Why is it easier to apologise without looking at someone?

- Eye contact can feel intense, so it is often easier to have difficult conversations when doing another activity or when side by side. Walking/hiking provides really good opportunities to talk.

Why do the Aberdares look like Scotland, even though they are in the middle of Africa?

- This is because of the high altitude. The higher the land, the thinner the air and so the colder it is. It may be hot and sunny during the day, but the temperature drops suddenly as soon as the sun goes down. Also, mountains cause air to move up over them, which often generates rain. The top of the Aberdares would have much higher rainfall and therefore look more lush than the surrounding countryside that is desperate for rain.

Many buffalo roam the Aberdare Mountains.

Chapter Seven

Wesley successfully climbs his first mountain and is involved in a car crash on the way home.

How did talking about triffids help the children to climb the hill?

- Henry knew that by telling them a story, he would distract them from the physical challenges of the climb. It helped Wesley to focus on something else, rather than his tiredness.

Why did Anna lose her temper when she was frightened?

- When people are frightened, stressed or in pain, they often find it difficult to be patient and are less tolerant of annoyances.

Why is it important to keep calm in a crisis?

- When things go wrong, it is often necessary to act quickly and to be able to problem-solve effectively. It is more difficult for the brain to think clearly if we become overwhelmed by emotion.

Why did Pete and Henry remain quite calm compared with the others when the car crashed?

- They are both soldiers and so are accustomed to unexpected and stressful events. They will have been trained to respond effectively in dangerous and frightening conditions and will have had direct experience of coping with life-threatening situations when on operational tours.

Why did Anna think 'Thank God for the Army'?

- In Kenya at the time, the emergency services were very limited and there were often serious traffic accidents and medical emergencies. The British Army provided medical support and vehicle recovery for all the British Army families living in Nanyuki.

Why did Wesley feel so good about comforting Anna and Isla?

- Wesley has received a lot of support from the Fosters since arriving in Kenya. It is not comfortable always to be the one needing help. He feels empowered because he remained calm after the crash and was able to rebalance the relationship by giving Anna and Isla support when they were upset.

Chapter Eight

Wesley meets Mr Morgan, Simon's father, in a meeting about the Mount Kenya trip. He realises that Mr Morgan bullies Simon.

How did Simon feel when his father kept interrupting the meeting?

- Simon is very aware that his father can be rude and is a bully. He is likely to have been embarrassed by his behaviour.

What do you think Simon's relationship with his father is like?

- It is very difficult. Mr Morgan is bitter about his own disappointments (which are explained later in the story) and so he puts huge pressure on Simon to succeed. Mr Morgan has fallen into a very negative way of interacting with Simon.

Why do you think Simon had not talked about his family at school?

- He feels humiliated by his father and doesn't want to talk about it. Despite his father's behaviour, Simon feels loyal to his parents (particularly his mother) and so doesn't want to criticise them in public. He also enjoys not having to think about his father at school, although he becomes nervous about tests as his father will be critical if Simon is not always top of the class.

Chapter Nine

The class start their climb of Mount Kenya and Simon talks about his father to the other boys.

Mount Kenya is on the Equator, so why is it so cold after dark?

- It is at a very high altitude where the air is thin and therefore does not retain the heat well. The sun is very intense during the day, which makes it warm, but as soon as it gets dark, which happens very suddenly at about 6 p.m., the temperature starts to plummet, so that often there is ice on the inside of the tents in the morning.

Why is it easier to talk about difficult topics in the dark?

- In the dark, the other boys could not see Simon, which made it easier for him to talk about his father without the others observing his reactions all the time.

What would it be like to have a parent who is always disappointed in you, no matter how well you do?

- It is likely to be very demoralising. Simon is constantly worried about how his father will react if he does not excel. It is not possible for Simon to distance himself from his father because he lives with him and sees him every day. Also, children often feel a very strong loyalty towards their parents, even when they repeatedly let the children down.

Chapter Ten

Isla and Simon dare each other to swim in an icy lake. The children then climb to their final campsite. Simon develops a severe headache in the evening.

Why was their last campsite barren, with no plants or wildlife?

- The terrain was so high, steep, rocky and cold that few plants grew there.

Why did Simon go to bed, rather than persevering to find Mr Mwangi?

- He was cold, exhausted and suffering from altitude sickness and so was not thinking clearly. If he had been in his right mind, he would have known that it was really important to tell a teacher about his headache.

The last campsite before the children try to reach the summit.

Why was the air so dry near the top of the mountain?

- Because the air was very thin and cold, it was unable to hold much moisture.

Chapter Eleven

The group starts the climb to the summit. Simon becomes confused due to altitude sickness, causing him and Wesley to fall down a cliff in the dark. Simon is badly injured, and Wesley helps him back to safety. Wesley talks about his mother in an attempt to keep Simon awake.

When they woke up, why was Simon's head in a fog? What should he have done?

- The altitude sickness was impairing his thinking. He should have immediately told a teacher because it can cause serious illness. The quickest way to relieve altitude sickness is to walk back down to a lower altitude or at least to stay at the same height and allow your body time to adjust. Climbing even higher to the summit was the worst thing to do.

After they fall down the cliff, why does Simon tell Wesley to talk to him, to keep him awake?

- Simon is very cold and in danger of suffering from hypothermia. He also has a head injury. If Simon falls asleep, his metabolism is likely to slow, which may make it even more difficult for him to stay warm.

What do you think caused Wesley's mum to be depressed?

- Several factors may have played a part. She did not have many friends and was very dependent on her parents for support when Wesley was born. Her parents died suddenly in quick succession, so she struggled with grief and the loss of her support network. She was very socially isolated and struggling to bring up a child alone. She was not working and so lacked the income and feelings of achievement and self-worth that often come through employment.

What do you think are the challenges of living with a parent who suffers from depression?

- In Wesley's case, his mother was not able to care for him consistently because there were days when she was so low that she was unable to get out of bed. There were times when she could not emotionally respond to Wesley in an appropriate way, which would mean that Wesley may feel that adults are unpredictable and difficult to trust.

There would have been times when Wesley had to care for himself and sometimes for his mother as well, when she was unable to function effectively. He also had fewer opportunities for fun and adventure due to his mother's mental health and their obesity.

Why did Wesley not tell anyone that his mother was missing for four days?

- He was hoping that she would return and that everything would be fine. Telling another adult made the problem real and he did not want to face up to the reality. Also, he was very isolated and did not have any close friends or adults that he trusted, so it was not easy for him to confide in someone.

Wesley was known as 'the fat boy' because that was his distinguishing feature. What do you think his other qualities might be?

- Wesley has shown huge perseverance and determination in sticking to his plan to lose weight and get fit. He has also shown flexibility and the ability to make friends and to adjust to a completely different life. In rescuing Simon, he demonstrates loyalty, quick thinking, selflessness, good problem solving, determination and leadership.

Why is Wesley's life better since he moved to Kenya? How does that make him feel?

- Wesley has lost a lot of weight and is now fitter and healthier. He is more able to interact with his peers and engage in activities with them. He finds the adventurous lifestyle in Kenya exciting. Although Pete is an inexperienced parent, he is able to look after Wesley effectively. Wesley is likely to feel guilty about thinking that his life has improved, because he loved his mother and with the right support her depression could have been treated.

Why does Simon need to get off the mountain as soon as possible?

• Simon is showing signs of altitude sickness. At a high altitude, the number of oxygen molecules per breath decreases, meaning that a person has to breathe faster and their heart must beat faster to gain enough oxygen. Symptoms typically improve by slowly descending to a lower altitude. Rising to higher altitudes can cause fluid to leak from the capillaries, causing a dangerous build-up of fluid in the lungs and brain. This can be life-threatening. In addition to this, Simon has had a serious fall, he has a head injury which is bleeding heavily and he is struggling to remain alert. He may have other internal injuries from the fall of which Wesley is not aware.

Why was it easy for Mr Mwangi to mistake Neil for Wesley during the climb to the summit?

• It was dark and they were all wrapped up against the cold, so it was hard to see their faces or hair colour. Also, Mr Mwangi was mentally and physically tired and so less observant than usual.

Chapter Twelve

Wesley helps Simon back to the campsite and with the help of the porters takes Simon back to Shipton's Hut where Pete has arranged for a helicopter to pick them up.

What gave Wesley the mental and physical strength to help Simon back to the campsite?

• Simon's life was in danger. Wesley knew he was the only person who could help and that he needed to take charge. People often find mental and physical strength to cope in difficult situations when other people are relying on them. Wesley will also have experienced the effects of adrenaline, which increases the functioning of the heart and lungs and reduces feelings of pain.

Why is it not possible to land a helicopter at the campsite?

- The air is so thin that the blades cannot get enough lift for the helicopter to take off, so it would be dangerous for a helicopter to land at such a high altitude.

Why does Wesley start telling Simon about triffids?

- He is worried that if Simon slips into unconsciousness, he might not wake up again. Therefore, he is keen to keep engaging with him. It also helps him to distract them both from the fear and discomfort of the situation and so makes the time pass more quickly.

How is Wesley likely to feel when the doctor arrives?

- He feels a huge sense of relief and that a great weight of responsibility is lifted from his shoulders. He is likely to become much more aware of his own exhaustion and pain, and may suddenly feel as though he does not have the energy to continue.

Chapter Thirteen

Wesley and Simon arrive at the hospital and Wesley stands up to Simon's father. They both receive medical care and Simon's mother thanks Wesley for saving Simon's life.

Do you think Wesley should have been so blunt with Simon's father?

- Wesley demonstrated considerable courage, loyalty and intelligence when he saved Simon's life. He was injured, exhausted and shocked, so it is not surprising that he loses his temper when Mr Morgan claims that the accident was Wesley's fault. Also, Wesley was right to stand up to Mr Morgan, who needed to know how that the pressure he had put on Simon had caused him to make bad decisions and put his life in danger.

How do you think Wesley felt after standing up to Mr Morgan?

- He probably felt quite proud for having defended himself and standing up to his friend's bully. When he calms down, he may feel a bit worried about having been so forthright and is probably keen not to see Simon's father again, in case he is angry.

What does Wesley mean when he says he has a fractured radius?

- He has a break in his radius. This is the larger bone in the lower arm. The ulna is the smaller bone next to it.

Chapter Fourteen

Wesley and Simon return to school, and Wesley wins an award.

Can you write Wesley's speech describing how he feels about his short time at school in Nanyuki?

Do you think it matters that he did not reach the summit of the mountain? Explain your answer.

- Wesley proved to everyone that he was capable of the climb. The only reason he did not reach the top was that he tried to help Simon. Saving Simon's life was a much greater achievement than reaching the top of the mountain.

How has Wesley's life changed for the better?

- He is no longer obese, meaning that his risks of ill health are greatly reduced.
- He has forged a positive relationship with his father.
- He has developed a group of friends and can take part in the same activities as his peers.

- Although he still misses his mother, the grief he experiences is now much less intense and less overwhelming.
- He has experienced a different life in Kenya which has broadened his knowledge and experience of the world.
- He has been physically and mentally challenged, and has discovered that he has many strengths including loyalty, determination and quick thinking in a crisis.
- He is happier than he was before.

Lake Michaelson where Simon and Isla break the ice before swimming.

Do you think Wesley will become obese again?

- It is unlikely, because he is very aware of how childhood obesity negatively affected his life. He has started to learn how to cook more healthy food and is leading a much more active life. However, he may need to be careful that he does not start turning to food for comfort if there is a time in his life when he feels persistently overwhelmed or depressed.

Epilogue

Simon and Wesley successfully climb Mount Kenya with their fathers.

How do you think Simon's relationship with his father has changed?

- Simon's father seems to have conquered many of his own demons. Climbing Mount Kenya with his leg injury will have been a huge challenge for him. He seems delighted to have achieved it with Simon. He has started to focus on what he is still able to do despite his injury, and being in a more positive frame of mind has helped to reduce the pain that he feels. Now that he has stopped trying to live his life through Simon's achievements, their relationship is much improved. The shock of Simon nearly dying has made Mr Morgan appreciate how much he loves his son.

How good do you think Wesley and Pete's relationship is by the end of the book?

- They have a really positive relationship and are finding out that they are quite similar both in stature and temperament. Both of them had difficult times as young children and so value the sense of family that they experience together. They really enjoy doing activities together. Their relationship is not perfect, and they both make mistakes. Pete never learns to be a good cook. Also, being a single father in the Army can be challenging as the job often requires soldiers to travel away from home for long periods, and Wesley has no grandparents or wider family support. However, they are both generally happy and draw support from their friends and colleagues.

Do you think it would be safe to slide down Mount Kenya on a tea tray?

- No!

An impala resting under an acacia tree.

6. Supporting Childhood Obesity

Something needs to be done about the obesity crisis and it needs to be done soon. The earlier that obese children can lose weight to the extent that they are no longer obese, the better it is for their future prospects. As childhood obesity has many causes, there is not going to be a single solution. Instead, a multi-factorial approach is required encompassing change on many levels.

For individuals, sustaining positive change is likely to be challenging, so obese children and their families may require some help during the process of losing weight. Resources to support childhood obesity are not widespread, and although dietician input is available, a more holistic approach including psychological support would be invaluable. Behaviour modification programmes for families may be available via the paediatric or child and adolescent mental health services, but unfortunately, at present, the funding isn't adequate to provide the frequency of input required or the availability for the numbers of children/families who would benefit from the service.

There are some specific childhood obesity clinics run by paediatricians which have multi-disciplinary teams, including doctors, dieticians, clinical psychologists, specialist nurses, social workers and exercise specialists: all of whom are crucial in breaking the cycle for individual children and helping them to maintain a normal, healthy weight. A Channel 4 documentary, *100 Kilo Kids*, follows one of the largest of these clinics, in Bristol. However, there aren't enough of these clinics in the UK to accommodate everyone who would benefit from them.

DOI: 10.4324/9781003207931-6

The Weight Set-Point

An emerging theme relating to weight management involves a person's weight set-point. This concept is explained in Jenkinson's book, *Why We Eat (Too Much)* (2020). The idea is that individuals' bodies are designed to keep their weight steady at a particular level. The weight set-point will vary from one individual to another and will be determined by several factors including the person's genes, diet and experiences throughout life. It has been suggested that even an expectant mother's diet and stress levels can affect her offspring's weight set-point.

Taubes (2011) highlights that it has recently become evident that babies are being born heavier than they used to, and are certainly heavier at six months compared with average weights 20 years ago. The influence of the mother's diet during pregnancy is thought to be a significant factor, and this is something that is emerging as a likely cause of childhood obesity. Therefore, clear advice to expectant mothers about diet may help to prevent some cases of childhood obesity.

For years, it has been assumed that a calorie-restricted diet is the best way to lose weight. However, there is evidence to show that when people go on calorie-restricted diets, the body's metabolism often slows down to conserve energy, because the body assumes that the person must be experiencing a famine situation. This means that people often lose weight at the start of a diet only to find that their rate of weight loss slows because their metabolism is trying to use energy as efficiently as possible. When they gradually relax their calorie restriction, people often put the weight back on and return to their previous weight. They bounce back to their set-point and may even end up a little heavier than before the diet. This is because the body assumes that it has just experienced a famine and so resets its hormones to store a little additional weight in case of future famine situations (Jenkinson, 2020). A similar process happens when people increase their levels of exercise, as the body will adapt its hunger and fat-regulation hormones to ensure there is enough energy available for the extra energy expenditure.

It is argued that in order to maintain weight loss, the body has to reset its set-point to a lower weight, and this requires re-tuning of the hormones and enzymes involved in the complex hunger and fat-regulation process. One of the ways of doing this is by changing what is eaten and moving away from highly processed foods to more fresh plant-based ingredients.

Intermittent fasting has become an increasingly popular way among adults to change the body's set-point, and there is evidence to support the effectiveness of this method. It involves only eating for a short part of each day, allowing time for insulin levels to drop and stay low for a longer period of time. There are currently very few scientific studies exploring this method that have involved children, and it may not be appropriate for children. Therefore, intermittent fasting is not currently advised as a weight-loss tool for children. This may change with time.

A goat nibbling a bush by the side of the road.

Change at the Individual Level

The following points should be considered when supporting obese children:

- For interventions to be successful, it is important for the child to recognise that being obese is a problem and to be motivated to lose weight. The need for weight loss and the physical and mental health issues that are associated with obesity should be explained.
- Children should be reassured that obesity is not their fault and that it can be rectified.
- Psychological support for the child (and family) should be prioritised to help them to sustain positive change and to address any difficulties the child has experienced due to stigma, bullying, anxiety and low mood.
- An appointment should be made with the child's GP so that any medical problems that might be contributing to the child's weight gain can be explored and ruled out.
- The GP practice can be involved in monitoring children's weight and referring to secondary care services as appropriate.
- Significant lifestyle changes are likely to be required for weight loss to be sustained; this needs to be taken on board by the child and also their family.
- Changes in activity levels will be required to improve overall health and fitness, rather than being seen as the sole method of weight loss. Increasing physical activity has many benefits that contribute to weight loss, such as improved mood, toning up muscles and body shape, opportunities to engage with others and success in achieving goals.
- Changes in diet may produce the greatest chance of success. The aim is to make long-term weight loss manageable. The goals need to be realistic and small, giving children a sense of achievement, which will boost their self-esteem, reinforce the positive changes made and maintain their motivation.

The Main Messages to Aid Weight Loss for a Child

- Weight loss is a complex process and not just about eating less and moving more. Sustained lifestyle changes are likely to be needed to reset the child's hunger and fat-regulation process.
- Minimise sugar, especially sugary drinks. This needs to be done carefully so that children don't feel they are being punished or deprived of food. Reducing snacks is a good place to start.
- Reduce refined carbohydrates such as white rice and white flour found in bread, pasta and pizza. Reducing portion size is a good first step, rather than suddenly eliminating a favourite food group.
- Increase plant-based foods, such as vegetables. There are lots of online resources that give great recipe ideas for vegetables. Please see the NHS Better Health: Healthier Families website (www.nhs.uk/healthier-families) for some recipe ideas.
- Changing to home-cooking of fresh ingredients rather than eating processed food can be difficult, especially for families who don't typically cook themselves, are busy and have limited budgets. So starting with simple recipes is sensible. It can also be helpful to encourage children to be involved in food preparation and for members of the family to share the cooking responsibility. It may take children time to adjust to eating food with less added sugar and salt. The challenges of this process need to be appreciated by everyone supporting the child and family.
- Keep insulin levels low by increasing the time between food and drink intakes – try to avoid snacks between meals.
- Being hungry does not mean that you have to eat – this is an important lesson for everyone to realise. It may take a while for children to become accustomed to being hungry before meals and to accept that this feeling is OK.
- Keep physically active; aim for some form of exercise every day, ideally outside.
- Encourage good sleeping habits and ensure the child is getting enough sleep, especially as a teenager. It is known that people who sleep well do better at losing weight, and that when people are tired, they often crave sugary food.

Change at the Family Level

- To address childhood obesity successfully, the family needs to be involved as much as the individual child. The family can provide positive support around the child.

- It is helpful if the whole family adopt changes in diet and lifestyle. As highlighted by Dr Hamilton-Shield from the Bristol Childhood Obesity Clinic in the Channel 4 documentary *100 Kilo Kids*, it is very challenging to get a child to cooperate with something that is not also being done by the rest of the family.

- It is important that all family members recognise that there is a problem with their child's weight. The whole family may also be overweight and therefore perceive this to be normal. The implications for their own and their child's health is something that needs to be acknowledged. This needs to be supported by messages from the wider community, provided in a non-judgemental way.

- Education for families, including pre-conception dietary education for prospective parents, is imperative to ensure the prevention of childhood obesity. There needs to be a focus on prevention, and education is the only way this can be achieved.

Change at the Community Level

There needs to be access to acceptable means of education for families and individuals. How this is delivered may vary depending on the target audience. For instance, using social media platforms might be effective for younger adults and adolescents. Community medical services could provide information to couples planning pregnancies, as well as those not necessarily planning a pregnancy but at risk of becoming pregnant.

Schools are a crucial part of the community, with ideal access to the children in their care, giving opportunities to provide accurate information, to change beliefs and support positive change. Schools are well placed to prioritise giving curriculum time to education about healthy lifestyles and could encourage activities such as cooking and outdoor pursuits by running clubs for both pupils and their parents. These would not only help to educate families but also provide opportunities for families to meet and socially interact, which would support mental health. There are many demands on school staff, and educational curriculums are already very busy, so it would be helpful for the government and education authorities to promote the importance of schools working to address childhood obesity and to support school staff in rising to the challenge.

Within communities, there needs to be the availability of appropriate, affordable ingredients for cooking healthy meals as well as opportunities for young people to take part in a variety of different physical activities. This is a priority for the Royal Society for Public Health (RSPH) which promotes 'Routing Out Childhood Obesity' (2021). The RSPH is calling for young children to have improved access to parks, changes to roads to promote walking and cycling, and limiting junk food outlets close to schools.

A documentary from Reboot USA (2016), **The Kids Menu**, focuses on problems with the availability of healthy eating choices in deprived areas. It discusses some incredible community programmes that have been developed in response to the obesity crisis. These include:

- **Urban Youth Education:** developing urban farms at which older school children can work, gaining valuable experience but also an appreciation of healthy own-grown foods, and increased availability of produce.
- **2 for 1 Schemes:** those deemed at health risk from obesity were given food stamps equivalent to doubling the healthy ingredients they can buy for their money – $2 worth of produce for the price of $1.
- **Prescriptions:** a community hospital provided free fruit and vegetables to those who needed them for home-cooking. The

provision of food was reviewed monthly and only continued if there was objective progress in weight loss.

These community schemes require time and commitment from community leaders as well as from the individuals who are running them. The benefits can be transformative, but the work invested in the initiatives should not be underestimated.

Changes Needed by Society

There is a need for society to change. This is likely to take time, but it is essential that change is initiated soon for an improvement in the current situation to occur. For substantial progress to be made, there needs to be overarching governmental recognition of the problem and increased investment in supporting obese children and preventing future cases of childhood obesity.

Small changes have happened over the last couple of decades – for instance, many supermarkets have moved sugary snacks away from their checkout areas to avoid temptation – but much larger steps need to be taken. The most recent NICE (National Institute of Clinical Excellence) medical guidance on obesity prevention is not up to date: it was written in 2006 and updated in 2015. So, at the time of writing, the updated guidance is six years out of date and there have been no significant improvements in the obesity problem since it was written.

The government, health professionals, church leaders and education authorities need to provide clear guidance to the population about what food we should be eating to prevent weight gain. Clear messages about the long-term impact of childhood obesity on physical and mental health should also be provided. Access to enjoyable alternatives to sugar and refined carbohydrates should be encouraged, with societal acceptance of these alternatives. This requires widespread change in people's thought patterns and beliefs about the impact of diet and lifestyle on our health. Progress can only be achieved with ongoing, multi-faceted interventions.

Solving the childhood obesity epidemic is going to take time, but it needs to be achieved.

The bridge that Wesley crosses on his way to school.

7. Conclusion

Childhood obesity is one of the greatest public health concerns of our time with far-reaching consequences, and yet the issue is complex and often poorly understood. The following key messages should be emphasised:

To support an obese child:

- Remember that the child is not to blame; children are influenced by their genes and the adults and society around them.
- A holistic approach is required to help the individual, with emotional as well as practical support.
- The whole family needs to accept that obesity is a problem and to support the changes required to solve it.

Prevention is as important as cure:

- We need to review **what** children are eating, as well as how much they eat.
- Reducing snacks and portion sizes (if appropriate) is a good place to start.
- Stopping sugary drinks and reducing intake of sugar, refined carbohydrates and highly processed foods appear to be the best options for weight loss.
- Increasing consumption of fresh produce and raising levels of activity is also helpful.

Education is paramount:

- Prevention of obesity needs to be a national focus, with education and availability of appropriate foodstuffs being top of the agenda.
- Lifestyle changes are needed by the family as a whole, not just the child who is struggling with obesity. Temporary calorie-restricted diets are unlikely to be the answer, so everyone needs to be aware of the alternatives.
- Messages about healthy eating and lifestyles need to be more consistent to reduce confusion.

DOI: 10.4324/9781003207931-7

The storybook ***Down Mount Kenya on a Tea Tray*** is intended to be an enjoyable read. It is hoped that, alongside this guide, it will help readers to understand some of the challenges faced by obese children and how they can be supported to overcome their difficulties. Childhood obesity is becoming better understood by scientists, but there continues to be an urgent need for the general population to recognise the complex web of issues that have led to the current obesity epidemic and how individuals, families, communities and societies can work together to promote healthier outcomes for our children.

Mount Kenya in the morning.

References

Anderson, S.E., Sacker, A., Whitaker, R.C. & Kelly, Y. (2017). Self-regulation and household routines at age three and obesity at age eleven: Longitudinal analysis of the UK Millennium Cohort Study. *International Journal of Obesity*, 41: 1459–1466. doi:10.1038/ijo.2017.94

Aparicio, E., Canals, J., Arija, V., De Henauw, S. & Michels, N. (2016). The role of emotion regulation in childhood obesity: Implications for prevention and treatment. *Nutrition Research Reviews*, 29: 17–29. doi:10.1017/S0954422415000153

Austin, J. & Marks, D (2009). Hormonal regulators of appetite. *International Journal of Paediatric Endocrinology*, 2009, 141753. doi:10.1155/2009/141753

Browne, N.T., Snethen, J.A., Greenberg, C.S., Frenn, M., Kilanowski, J.F., Gance-Cleveland, B., Burke, P.J., & Lewandowski, L. (2021). When pandemics collide: The impact of COVID-19 on childhood obesity. *Journal of Pediatric Nursing*, 56: 90–98. doi:10.1016/j.pedn.2020.11.004

Channel 4 (2020). *100 Kilo Kids: Obesity SOS*.

Childhood Obesity Foundation (2019). What is childhood obesity? https://childhoodobesityfoundation.ca/what-is-childhood-obesity (accessed March 2021).

Danese, A. & Tan, M. (2014). Childhood maltreatment and obesity: Systematic review and meta-analysis. *Molecular Psychiatry*, 19(5): 544–554.

Fung, J. (2016). *The Obesity Code: Unlocking the Secrets of Weight Loss*. Scribe, London.

Graziano, P.A., Kelleher, R., Calkins, S.D., Keane, S.P. & Brien, M.O. (2013). Predicting weight outcomes in preadolescence: The role of toddlers' self-regulation skills and the temperament dimension of pleasure. *International Journal of Obesity*, 37: 937–942. doi:10.1038/ijo.2012.165

Hemmingsson, E., Johansson, K. & Reynisdottir, S. (2014). Effects of childhood abuse on adult obesity: A systematic review and meta-analysis. *Obesity Reviews*, 15(11): 882–893 https://doi.org/10.1111/obr.12216

HM Government (2020). Childhood obesity: Applying 'All Our Health'. www.gov.uk/government/publications/childhood-obesity-applying-all-our-health/childhood-obesity-applying-all-our-health (accessed February 2021).

HM Government (2017). Childhood Obesity: A Plan for Action. https://assets.publishing.service.gov.uk/government/uploads/system/uploads/attachment_data/file/546588/Childhood_obesity_2016__2__acc.pdf (accessed January 2021).

Hope, S., Micali, N., Deighton, J. & Law, C. (2019). Maternal mental health at 5 years and childhood overweight or obesity at 11 years: Evidence from the UK Millennium Cohort Study. *International Journal of Obesity*, 43(1): 43–52.

Jenkinson, A. (2020). *Why We Eat (Too Much): The New Science of Appetite*. Penguin Life, UK.

Leppert, B., Junge, K.M., Röder, S., Borte, M., Stangl, G.I., Wright, R.J., Hilbert, A., Lehmann, I. & Trump, S. (2018). Early maternal perceived stress and children's BMI: Longitudinal impact and influencing factors. *BMC Public Health*, 18(1): 1211.

Momin, S.R., Mackenzie, K.S., Buckley, S., Buist, N., Ghandi, M., Hair, A., Hughes, S., Hodges, K., Lange, W., Papaioannou, M., Phan, M., Waterland, R. & Wood, A. (2020). Rationale and design of the Baylor Infant Twin Study – A study assessing obesity-related risk factors from infancy. *Obesity Science and Practice*, 7(1): 63–70. doi:10.1002/osp4.463

National Cancer Institute (2017). Obesity and cancer. www.cancer.gov/about-cancer/causes-prevention/risk/obesity/obesity-fact-sheet (accessed April 2021).

NICE (National Institute of Clinical Excellence) (2015). Obesity prevention: Clinical guideline [CG43]. www.nice.org.uk/guidance/cg43 (accessed March 2021).

Pont, S.J., Puhl, R., Cook, S.R., Slusser, W., Section on Obesity, The Obesity Society (2017). Stigma experienced by children and adolescents with obesity. *Pediatrics*, 140(6), e20173034. doi:10.1542/peds.2017-3034

Rankin, J., Matthews, L., Cobley, S., Han, A., Sanders, R., Wiltshire, H.D. & Baker, J.S. (2016). Psychological consequences of childhood obesity: Psychiatric comorbidity and prevention. *Adolescent Health, Medicine and Therapeutics*, 7: 125–146. doi:10.2147/AHMT.S101631

Rankin, J., Matthews, L., Cobley, S., Han, A., Sanders, R., Wiltshire, H. & Baker, J. (2016). Psychological consequences of childhood obesity: Psychiatric comorbidity and prevention. *Adolescent Health, Medicine and Therapeutics*, 7: 125–146. doi:10.2147/AHMT.S101631.

Reboot USA (2016) The Kids Menu, *Reboot USA*.

Roberts, C.A. (2021). Physical and psychological effects of bariatric surgery on obese adolescents: A review. *Frontiers in Pediatrics*, 8. doi:10.3389/fped.2020.591598

Royal Society for Public Health (2019). Routing Out Childhood Obesity. www.rsph.org.uk/our-work/policy/obesity/routing-out-childhood-obesity.html (accessed September 2021).

Rupp, K. & McCoy, S.M. (2019). Bullying perpetration and victimization among adolescents with overweight and obesity in a nationally representative sample. *Childhood Obesity*, 15(5): 323–330. doi:1089/chi.2018.0233

Russell-Mayhew, S., McVey, G., Bardick, A. & Ireland (2012). Depression, obesity, eating behavior, and physical activity. *Journal of Obesity*, 2012: 281801. doi:10.1155/2012/281801

Sahoo, K., Sahoo, B., Choudhury, A., Sofi, N., Kumar, R. & Bhadoria, A. (2015). Childhood obesity: Causes and consequences. *Journal of Family Medicine and Primary Care*, 4(2): 187–192.

Schlam, T.R., Wilson, N.L., Shoda, Y., Mischel, W. & Ayduk, O. (2013). Preschoolers' delay of gratification predicts their body mass 30 years later. *The Journal of Pediatrics*, 162(1): 90–93. doi:10.1016/j.jpeds.2012.06.049

Scott, H., Biello, S.M. & Woods, H.C. (2019). Social medial use and adolescent sleep patterns: Cross-sectional findings from the UK millennium cohort study. *BMJ Open*, 9(9). doi:10.1136/bmjopen-2019-031161.

Sleddens, E.F., Gerards, S.M., Thijs, C., de Vries, N.K. & Kremers, S.P. (2011). General parenting, childhood overweight and obesity-inducing behaviors: A review. *International Journal of Pediatric Obesity*, 6(2-2): e12–27.

Smith, J.D., Fu, E. & Kobayashi, M.A. (2020). Prevention and management of childhood obesity and its psychological and health comorbidities. *Annual Review of Clinical Psychology*, *16*, 351–378. doi:10.1146/annurev-clinpsy-100219-060201

Smith, J.D., St. George, S.M. & Prado, G. (2017). Family-centered positive behavior support interventions in early childhood to prevent obesity. *Child Development*, 88(2): 427–435. doi:10.1111/cdev.12738.

Storz M.A. (2020). The COVID-19 pandemic: An unprecedented tragedy in the battle against childhood obesity. *Clinical and Experimental Pediatrics*, *63*(12): 477–482. doi:10.3345/cep.2020.01081

Stout, S.A., Espel, E.V., Sandman, C.A., Glynn, L.M. & Davis, E.P. (2015). Fetal programming of children's obesity risk. *Psychoneuroendocrinology*, 53: 29–39.

Taubes, G. (2011). *Why We Get Fat and What to Do About It.* Anchor Books, New York.

Vanderpump, M.P.J. (2011). The epidemiology of thyroid disease. *British Medical Bulletin*, 99(1): 39–51.

Wardle, J., Carnell, S., Haworth, C.M. & Plomin, R. (2008). Evidence for a strong genetic influence on childhood adiposity despite the force of the obesogenic environment. *The American Journal of Clinical Nutrition*, 87(2): 398–404. doi: 10.1093/ajcn/87.2.398

World Health Organization (2021a) Obesity and overweight. www.who.int/news-room/fact-sheets/detail/obesity-and-overweight (accessed August 2021).

World Health Organization (2021b) Child growth standards. www.who.int/tools/child-growth-standards/standards (accessed January 2021).

References

World Health Organization, Regional Office for Europe (2017). World Obesity Day: Understanding the social consequences of obesity. www.euro. who.int/en/health-topics/noncommunicable-diseases/mental-health/ news/news/2017/10/world-obesity-day-understanding-the-social-consequences-of-obesity (accessed August 2021).